T0160916

ABC

Swiss

Bergli Books has been supported by the
Swiss Federal Office of Culture with a structural
grant for the years 2021–2025.

ABC Swiss
ISBN: 978-3-03869-125-9

First edition: November 2022
Deposit copy in Switzerland: November 2022
Printed in the Czech Republic

© 2022 Bergli Books
an imprint of HELVETIQ (Helvetiq Sàrl)
Mittlere Strasse 4 CH-4056 Basel, Switzerland

ABC

Swiss

Niels Blaesi

A

Come on!
See what's hiding in the ALPHORN!

B

And blow bubbles in the BLAUSEE.

But be careful, because with a whoosh!
your CERVELAT is gone.

D

On the DUFOURSPITZE
you are the tallest of them all.

E

Don't forget to save the last sip of water
for the EDELWEISS.

F

If you get hungry,
you can smell FONDUE from far, far away.

G

And if you look carefully,
the past is hiding in the GLACIER.

H

But time flies
when HEIDI and Peter are together.

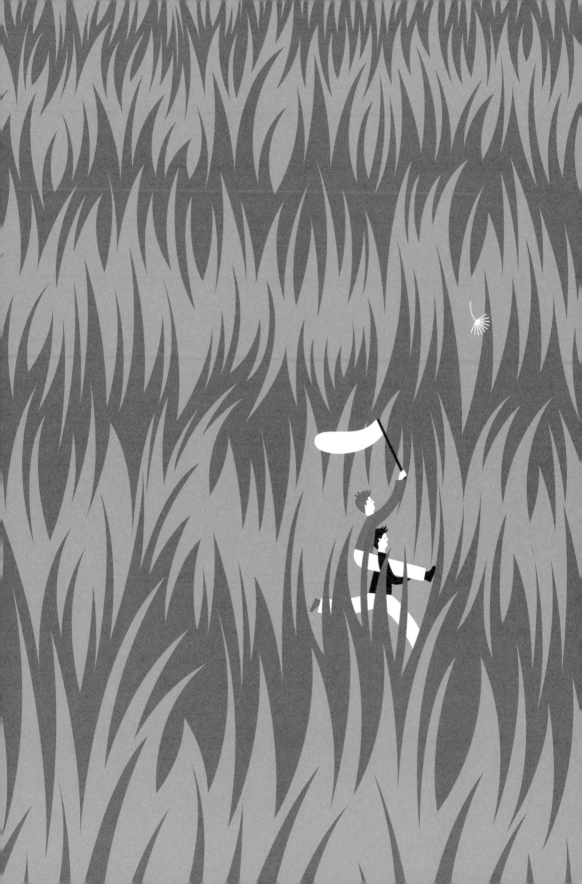

I

When you get bored,
you'll get shown all around INTERLAKEN.

J

Far away in Geneva,
the JET D'EAU is so very high.

K

And in KLEWENALP
you can zoom up and down,

L

before stopping in at LUCERNE'S carnival.

M

If you want some peace and quiet, no one will find you at the church in MOGNO.

N

But don't forget to bring home something
to remember your ride up the NIESEN.

By the way, everyone has heard of OLTEN,
but no one knows what it looks like.

P

On PIZ BERNINA
you can hear the snowflakes falling.

But you may have company
if you dig for QUARTZ.

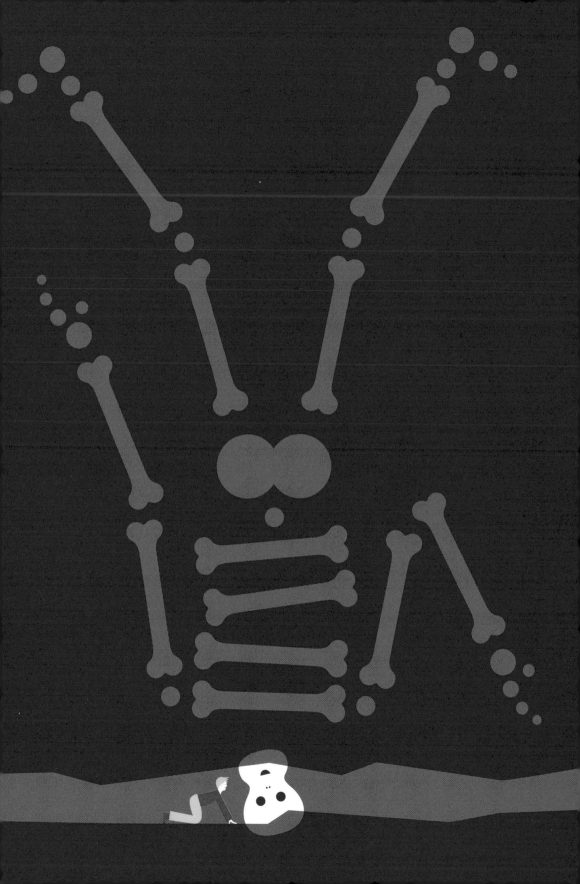

R

Your umbrella won't help you
at the RHINE FALLS.

S

Though with SKIS on your feet,
you'll be as fast as lightning.

T

Almost there!
The sun is waiting in TICINO!

U

If you're not afraid, you may want
to spit from URI'S Devil's Bridge.

V

And take a break. The VITRA
Wiggle Side Chair is so comfortable.

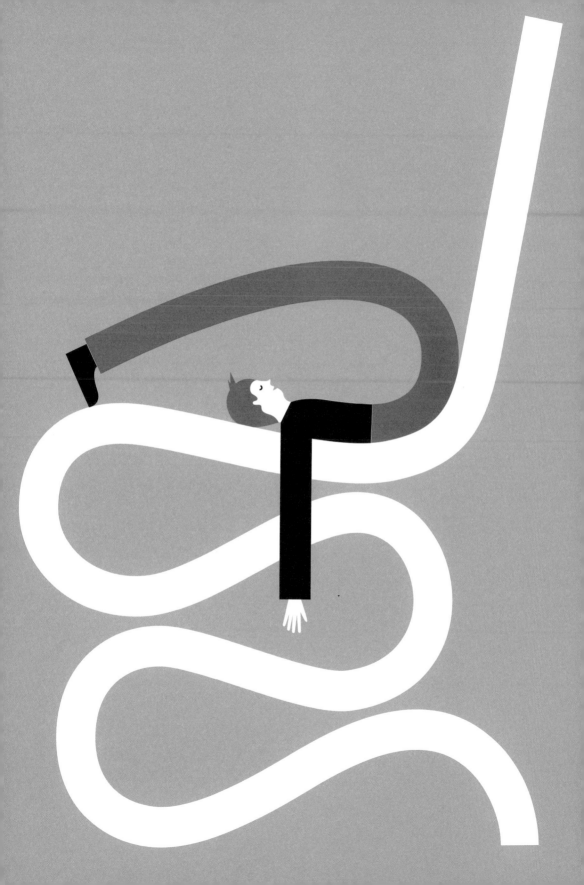

W

Even WILLIAM TELL had bad days.

X

If you're looking for Switzerland,
X marks the spot.

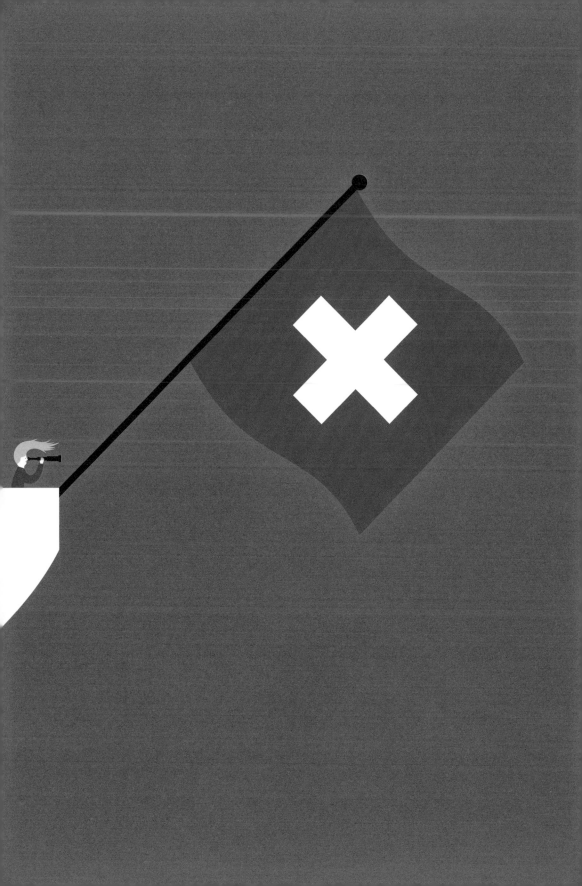

Y

And before it's too late, catch the last rays of sunshine at the beaches of Yvonand.

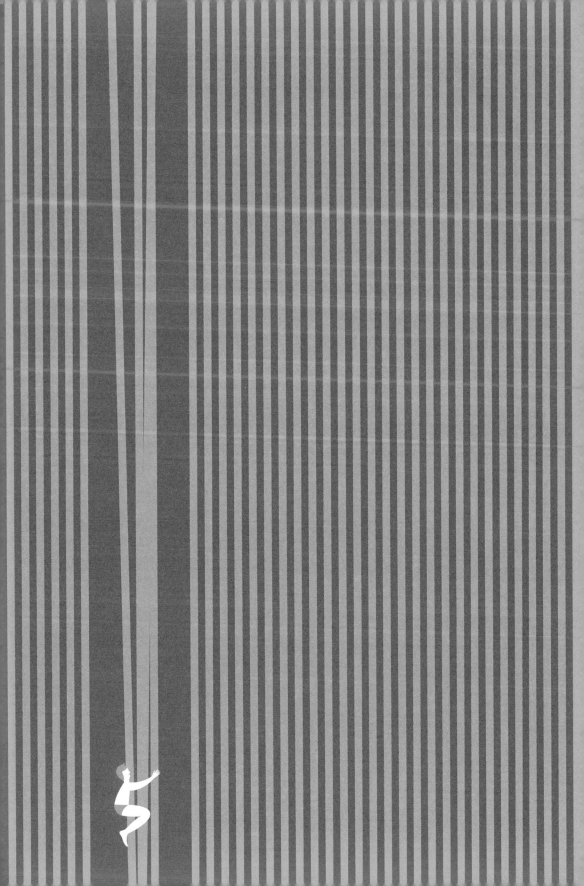

Z

Last of all, ZURICH begins with Z.

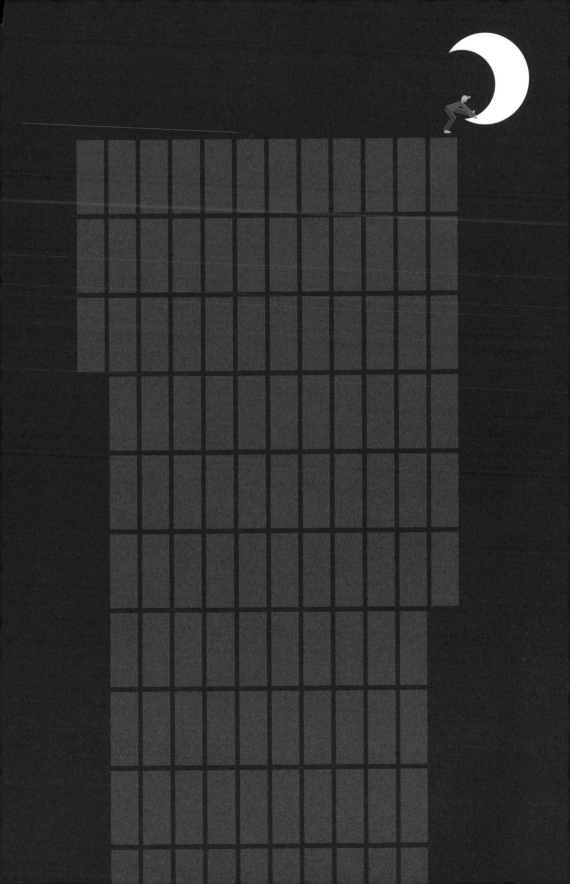

ALPHORN
Musical instrument

BLAUSEE
Alpine lake in the Bernese Oberland

CERVELAT
A sausage

DUFOURSPITZE
Highest point in Switzerland

EDELWEISS
An alpine flower

FONDUE
A way to eat cheese

GLACIER
Crevasses are huge cracks in glaciers

HEIDI
The main character in the famous children's book by Johanna Spyri (1827–1901)

INTERLAKEN
A tourist destination in the Bernese Oberland

JET D'EAU
A fountain in Geneva

KLEWENALP
A hiking and ski paradise in Canton Nidwalden

LUZERNE
One of Switzerland's favorite carnivals

MOGNO
A church in the Ticino village of Mogno

NIESEN
Next to the Niesen funicular railway is the world's longest staircase

OLTEN
One of Switzerland's most important rail junctions

PIZ BERNINA
The highest peak in Canton Graubünden

QUARTZ
A crystal found in the mountains

RHINE FALLS
A waterfall in Canton Schaffhausen

SKIS
You need them for one of Switzerland's favorite sports

TICINO
The Gotthard Tunnel connects Canton Ticino with the rest of Switzerland

URI
The legend of the Devil's Bridge takes place in the Schöllenen Gorge

VITRA
A Swiss company designing furniture with a museum in Weil am Rhein

WILLIAM TELL
A Swiss folk hero

X
The Swiss flag is a cross

YVONAND
A village on Lake Neuchâtel

ZURICH
The biggest city in Switzerland